Dive into Danger

Library Learning Information

Idea Store® Bow
1 Gladstone Place
Roman Road
London E3 5ES

020 7364 4332

Created and managed by
Tower Hamlets Council

Published in 2002 by:
Nelson Thornes Ltd
Delta Place
27 Bath Road
CHELTENHAM
GL53 7TH
United Kingdom

02 03 04 05 06 / 10 9 8 7 6 5 4 3 2 1

A catalogue record for this book is available from the British Library

ISBN 0-7487-6688-X

Cover illustration by Martin Berry
Page make-up by Tech-Set, Gateshead

Printed in Croatia by Zrinski

1

My name is Roger Chapman. I used to work on a mini-sub called Pisces 3. There was just room for me and my mate, Roger Mallinson. Our job was to inspect underwater cables and rigs, things like that.

Our sub was loaded with gadgets. It had a robot arm outside to grab things. It also had a strong light so we could see what we were doing. Inside there were oxygen bottles and something called a 'scrubber'.

Everyone breathes out carbon dioxide. This is bad air. The scrubber was there to 'scrub' the air clean. It was used about once every 90 minutes. We could also use oxygen from the bottles to keep the air fresh. In a sub there's only so much oxygen. You can't pipe more down from the surface.

A big battery gave the sub all the power we needed to stay under water for ten hours. We kept food and drink on board. A two-way radio kept us in contact with our ship, Voyager.

Pisces 3 was winched into the water from Voyager. A strong cable was fixed to the sub and it was gently lowered into the sea. Then the battery took over.

A lot of people would hate working in a sub. They couldn't stand being cut off from the outside world in a little metal box. But I enjoyed my job. I found it exciting. And working with Roger was great. What he didn't know about the sub wasn't worth knowing.

On 29 August 1973 we were 500 metres under the Irish Sea. We were using the robot arm to bury a phone cable. The cable had to be buried because fishermen's nets could get hooked on it. That could be dangerous.

It was 9.30 am. We'd been down for nine hours. We were tired and hungry. When the radio call came from Voyager, we weren't sorry. We took the sub close to the surface. A diver from the ship fixed a line on to the sub ready for us to be pulled out of the water.

The lift usually took about 45 minutes. But not this time. This time it took much, much longer.

We were lucky to get out at all.

2

The ship began to winch us up. Things were going well. Then, without warning, an alarm began to screech. At the same time the sub tipped over and started to sink.

As we went down we were thrown all over the place, along with our things. We were going down fast. The depth gauge was reading nearly 30 metres. We were dropping like a stone.

I guessed what had happened. One of the tanks on the sub had flooded. There must have been a tonne of water in the tank instead of air.

Suddenly we jerked to a stop. Voyager's lifting line had stopped us from dropping any further. But I knew there were problems.

'Voyager will never hold us,' I said to Roger. 'Our tank's flooded. We're too heavy. The line's not strong enough.'

Roger didn't need me to tell him that. He already knew. A voice came over the radio. 'Pisces 3. This is Voyager. We're sending some divers down. They'll fix another lifting line on you. Then we'll try to pull you up again. Hold on.'

The radio died. We waited in silence. There was nothing we could do. But the divers never had chance to get to us. There was a loud crack. The line had snapped. Roger's face turned white as we began to plunge to the seabed. He was near the depth gauge and called out the readings.

We were already 150 metres down and dropping fast. If we hit the seabed hard we'd be lucky to survive. My mind was racing. What could we do?

I found the power switch and flicked it off. If we struck the bottom with the power on we might catch fire. I caught sight of the depth gauge. It was spinning like a fruit machine. We were down to 250 metres and still falling out of control.

300 . . . 350 . . . 400. We were scrambling around in a mad hunt for something soft to lie on. We stripped the cushions from the seats. We had to put something between us and the sides of the sub. Sleeping bags. Anything to soften the blow.

I fought against panic. It seemed to rise in my throat. Down and down we went. It seemed to take ages. I closed my eyes and waited for us to hit the bottom.

3

I heard the boom and shot forward. We'd hit the seabed. For a minute we didn't speak. It was pitch black inside the sub. I thought we'd lost our power. I held my breath and switched on. The controls lit up. Everything was working! The depth gauge read 525 metres. There was more than half a kilometre of water above our heads.

Roger said, 'Listen. Can you hear that?'

A faint hissing sound came from somewhere in the sub. I said, 'It's the main oxygen bottle. It's leaking.'

We hunted around for the bottle. The sub was standing on its tail. Everything had been thrown around. It was like being in an upside-down room. The things that should have been on the wall were now on the floor. The oxygen bottle was buried.

It was Roger who found it. He turned the valve and the hissing stopped. We breathed a sigh of relief.

'Is the scrubber all right?' he asked.

If the scrubber was smashed we were in deep trouble. It was the size of a big biscuit tin and took the carbon dioxide out of the air. Without the scrubber our air would poison us.

My hands were shaking as I checked the scrubber. My heart felt like it was going to thump a hole in my chest. I could have wept for joy. It was okay!

At that moment the radio crackled into life. It was Voyager. 'Pisces 3, are you all right?'

'Yes, Voyager. We're okay.'

'Anyone hurt?'

'No. We're both fine.'

'Sit tight. We'll soon have you out of there.'

Voyager had very strong lifting gear. If they could send divers to fix a line on us they could pull us to safety. But divers from Voyager couldn't swim down that far. We were too deep. Only another mini-sub could help us.

The radio came on again. 'This is Voyager to Pisces 3. We have to pick up another sub. We have to go to Cork. We'll be as fast as we can. Don't worry. We won't let you down.'

Cork is a town in Ireland. It was 240 kilometres away. Voyager had to get there, load up and get back. It would take more than 30 hours if all went well. But the weather forecast was bad. It could take much longer.

I kept my thoughts to myself as Voyager pulled away. We could hear the 'thump-thump' of its engines fading into the distance. We felt sad and alone. We were prisoners in our small, dark cell.

Between us and freedom were over 500 metres of cold water. It was like being at the bottom of the world's tallest building. We were 150 floors down with no lift in sight.

We tried to stay calm. We had a good supply of oxygen. We had some food and plenty of water. All we had to do was wait. Voyager would find a way to get us up again. The crew wouldn't let us down. They were all good men. They knew every trick in the book. They'd get us back safely. All we had to do was wait.

But it was hard to stay cheerful. I was hot and tired and shaking with shock. I was worried, too. I thought we might have broken a seal when we hit the seabed. I could feel drops of water falling on my face. I thought we'd sprung a leak.

I touched the water and licked my fingers. It wasn't salty. It was condensation, not sea water.

We'd hit the bottom, but we hadn't sprung a leak. We had power and the scrubber was still working. We'd been lucky so far. We'd won some time.

As the minutes ticked by, time became the most important thing in the world to us.

4

I stared through the porthole into the dark water. We didn't say much. Worries crowded in on my mind. Would another mini-sub find us? We were very tiny and the sea was very big. And what about the air? As every second passed we were using up more of our life-giving oxygen. It wouldn't last for ever.

We tried to make ourselves comfortable. It wasn't easy. The sub was very cramped. The cabin was only a couple of metres across. We had to lie down to look out of the ports. There was just enough room to stand.

We made a bed out of seats. We moved everything we might need close to the bed. We didn't want to move around. Moving about would use up more oxygen. We switched off the lights to save the battery. Then we lay down in the darkness. We tried to lie very still. We didn't talk much. Talking cost oxygen. We had to use as little oxygen as possible.

Once every hour we switched on the scrubber. We kept it running for 10 minutes. We didn't know how long we'd be at the bottom of the sea. The air hadn't been fresh at the end of our shift when the line snapped. We'd have to use the scrubber more often to clean up the air. Even with it working, the longer we were under the sea the worse the air would get.

The scrubber hummed like a hoover. It was a comforting sound. When it wasn't running we could hear all kinds of noises. The sub creaked as it sank into the mud. The deep isn't silent. It's full of sounds.

By about 10 o'clock that night we both had a headache. The air was getting worse. I turned to Roger. 'It's the scrubber,' I said. 'It needs a new filter.'

'I'll do it,' Roger said.

We always kept spare filters in the sub. They are about the size of a big coffee jar. When a filter got clogged up, we changed it.

It took him a long time. He worked slowly and carefully. Our lives depended on the scrubber.

We slept. But we had to wake up once every hour to work the scrubber. We had a couple of timers. They were like little alarm clocks. We set them before we went to sleep and prayed one of us would wake up. We also had to open the oxygen bottle for a few seconds. We needed this 'shot' of oxygen to stay alive.

It was a long night. The sub was cold and pitch black. Our sleep was heavy, but one of us always heard the timer and woke up to work the scrubber. The hours passed slowly. My watch told me it was Thursday. We knew nothing would happen before midnight. We hoped Voyager would be back by then.

5

It was no use pretending. We were in a tight spot. I was glad I was with Roger. He knew the sub inside out.

We tried to relax. We didn't talk much. Every move meant we'd use some oxygen. Without oxygen we wouldn't be around long. The build-up of bad air soon made it hard to sit up or even talk. Roger got cramp in his legs.

He began to feel ill. I couldn't see why. We'd run the scrubber every hour. We'd changed the filters. Then I saw what was wrong. We were sleeping with our feet higher than our heads. Our hearts were having to work too hard. We had to move our beds around. Even this simple job took half an hour. We were getting very tired.

It was 9 o'clock on Thursday night before we got the radio message. 'Pisces 3. This is Voyager. We're four hours away. Coming at full speed. Hold on.'

It was great news. Hearing a friendly voice was the most amazing thing in the world. We'd been waiting for hours in the cold and the dark. The radio message was like a ray of warm sunshine.

Voyager told us they'd picked up two mini-subs in Cork – Pisces 2 and Pisces 5. Pisces 2 had been flown in from the North Sea. Pisces 5 had come all the way from Canada.

We learnt there were other ships nearby, all offering help. We bucked up a lot. We even got a message from the Queen Elizabeth wishing us luck. At first we thought it was from *the* Queen. Then Voyager told us it was from the liner, QE2. It had passed close by on its way to America. We couldn't believe how much people cared. It really helped us to cope with what lay ahead.

At 11.20pm we got another call from Voyager. 'Pisces 3. We have good news. Pisces 2 will be with you shortly.'

Just after midnight, Pisces 2 was lowered into the water. It was going to bring another line down to us from Voyager. It would use its robot arm to fix the line to our hull. Voyager could then lift us to the surface.

It took Pisces 2 over an hour to reach the seabed. But it was a long way from us. We could tell from its sonar 'pings' it was more than a kilometre away. My heart sank. How long would it be before we were found?

That wasn't the only problem. I heard Pisces 2 radio Voyager to say they had a leak. It was only a small leak. But it would be too risky for Pisces 2 to stay on the seabed. At that depth the weight of water is like having a bus full of people on your hand.

Our spirits sank. We lay in the darkness without speaking. What else could go wrong? We listened in silence as Pisces 2 made its way back to the top. We'd thought we were going to be rescued. We'd got excited and this had pushed up the carbon dioxide level. At about 5 o'clock in the morning I put another filter in the scrubber. The bad air made us both feel very tired.

Some time later, Voyager radioed again. 'Slight problem with Pisces 2. Will send Pisces 5 down as soon as it's ready.' Once again, our spirits rose. Help was on the way. All we had to do was wait.

Pisces 5 arrived on the seabed at just after 6 o'clock on Friday morning. It searched for us for hours but couldn't find us. Its batteries were nearly dead. It had to go back up to the surface.

It would be lowered again soon. All we could do was wait. And hope.

6

By now the rescue was front-page news. TV crews came from all over the world. They wanted to know about Pisces 3. How had the accident happened? Who was trapped in the sub? Would they get out alive?

There were many small boats in the area. We could hear the throb of their engines. The noise made it hard for us to talk to Voyager. Voyager's captain told the boats to move away. Most did. But one stayed. The newsmen on board wouldn't budge until they had the full story.

When Pisces 5 got back to the surface it had a problem with its compass. The crew worked hard to fix it. It took until 11.00 am on Friday before Pisces 5 was ready to dive again. By this time we'd been at the bottom for 50 hours.

Voyager came on the radio. 'Pisces 3. This is Voyager. Pisces 5 is on its way down.'

'Third time lucky,' I said to Roger.

He didn't reply. He was in a lot of pain. The carbon dioxide was building up in his body and making him very ill. He reached out for my hand.

'Pisces 5 is on the way,' I told him. 'It won't be long now.'

We weren't hungry. But we ate some biscuits. We had to keep our strength up.

I tried to sound cheerful. But I felt very low. The bad air was making me sluggish. I was careless and dropped one of the timers. It fell to the bottom of the sub. It took me ages to find it. I was angry with myself. I'd used more oxygen. Oxygen was our lifeline. I tied the timer to my wrist. I wasn't going to lose it again.

Now a radio call from Pisces 5 broke the silence. 'Pisces 3, we're on the seabed.'

It sounded very close. I thought my ears were playing tricks. I looked out of the port but there was no sign of its lights.

The radio crackled again. 'Keep talking to us, Pisces 3. Sing us a song. We'll find you. Just keep singing.'

I didn't feel like singing. It was the last thing I wanted to do. But I did. I sang a made-up song. A song with silly words and a silly tune. I sang the song in the darkness with my mate in pain by my side.

We were playing a deadly game of hide and seek. We were hiding. Pisces 5 was seeking. If they didn't find us we'd die. We only had so much oxygen. We only had one more filter for the scrubber. The battery wouldn't last for ever. They had to find us.

Suddenly we saw a light through the port! We sat up and pressed our faces against the misty glass. Pisces 5's spotlights looked as bright as the sun to our tired eyes. I turned to Roger and grinned. Tears were streaming down his face. It was a moment of pure joy. A moment I will never forget.

We decided to toast our good luck. We opened our last can of lemonade and had a few sips each.

Pisces 5 radioed to us. 'We can see you, Pisces 3! Hang on.'

We could do nothing now but wait. Some of the world's top underwater experts were working on the rescue. If they couldn't save us, nobody could.

I fixed the last of the filters into the scrubber. It was a simple job. It should have taken me five minutes. I was so weak it took me nearly an hour. I checked the oxygen bottle. If we were careful it would last 24 hours.

Pisces 5 was behind us now. It was using its robot arm to hook the lifting line on to our sub. It stirred up clouds of mud from the seabed. It looked like a ghost as it moved around.

It took 20 minutes to fix the line. It was the longest 20 minutes of my life. Then things went wrong again.

7

The crew of Pisces 5 had worked hard to fix the line on to us. But they didn't get it right. The line wasn't fixed properly. It began to float away. Pisces 5 grabbed it just in time. The line would have drifted back up to the surface.

The minutes ticked by. We saw Pisces 5's lights in the water as they tried again. At last we heard the lifting hook snap into place. 'This is it,' I thought. 'We're on our way up.'

Our hopes rose. But not for long. Pisces 5 radioed the bad news. 'The hook's in the wrong place. Stand by, Pisces 3. We'll try again.'

They'd fixed the line. But not to the right part of our sub. They'd fixed it to a weak spot. If Voyager tried to lift us, we'd break up. Pisces 5 tried again and again. We counted the minutes. What was happening? What was the problem? We hadn't slept for over 60 hours. We couldn't think straight.

It was 2.30 on Saturday morning when Pisces 5 came on the radio. 'Sorry, Pisces 3. We're running out of power. We've got to rest the batteries. Our main battery's nearly flat.'

They had to stop work. The robot arm needed power. They had to turn off their spotlights. Pisces 5 had to save enough power to get back up to the surface. If it didn't, it would be trapped on the bottom, too.

Once again the darkness seemed to close in on us. Pisces 5 had given us hope. We'd watched its lights through the portholes. We'd felt less alone. I think this was the moment when I nearly gave up hope. Pisces 5 was next to us on the seabed. Pisces 2 was being mended.

I asked Roger how he was feeling.

'A bit better,' he said.

I slept for a few hours, while he worked the scrubber. It was very cold, but the air was better. Suddenly I woke up.

'What's that noise?' I said.

We stared at each another. We were dazed. We didn't have the strength to think. We could hear a loud noise, close by. What was it?

'It's Pisces 5,' said Roger. 'They're testing their sonar. Their batteries must be okay now. They're getting ready to have another go at fixing the line.'

I looked out of the port. I could just make out its lights through the clouds of mud. The other sub radioed. 'Pisces 5 to Pisces 3. Stand by. We're going to try again.'

We said nothing. We hardly dared breathe. We could feel Pisces 5 bumping our sub as it worked. It was just a few metres away. I thought about the two pilots in Pisces 5. Doing all they could to save us. Putting their own lives at risk. Racing against time. Then we got a radio message that made our hearts sink.

'Sorry, Pisces 3. We're nearly out of power. We can't fix the line. We must surface.'

I didn't want Pisces 5 to leave us. I knew its pilots felt the same. But they had no choice. They had to go. They'd been on the seabed for 13 hours. They were very tired. There was no point putting their lives at risk.

I radioed back. 'Good luck, Pisces 5.'

'You too,' came the reply.

'See you soon,' I managed to say. 'Safe trip.'

I heard Pisces 5 making its way back to the top. It would soon be back, but by then it might be too late.

As it rose through the water, Voyager's crew were racing to mend Pisces 2.

We settled down to wait. It was dark and cold. We drifted in and out of sleep. We lost all track of time. I was no longer sure what day it was. We were cold and damp. There was a lot of condensation in the cabin. We kept close so we could share our body heat.

We tried to sleep. Every hour, the timer woke us with a jolt. Time to turn on the scrubber. Time for another 'shot' of oxygen.

I thought about my wife, June. I wondered if I'd ever see her again. The long hours of waiting must have been even worse for Roger. He had three young children at home.

At last, Voyager radioed. 'We've had an unmanned sub flown in from America. And Pisces 2 is ready to dive. The weather's a bit rough up here. Don't worry. We'll soon have you home and dry.'

Their cheerful message made us feel better. At last, things were going our way. But our hopes were dashed as Pisces 2 was lowered into the sea.

Voyager radioed down. 'Voyager to Pisces 3. We still have a problem. Pisces 2 is taking in water. Nothing too bad. We'll send it down as soon as we can.'

There was also a problem with CURV, the unmanned sub.

Anything that could go wrong had gone wrong. I felt as if we were riding a roller coaster. High hopes one minute. Down in the dumps the next. Would we ever see daylight again?

8

By now we'd been trapped for over 70 hours. We were running out of time. Soon there'd be no power to run the scrubber. And what about the oxygen? I checked the bottle. We had 12 hours left. If we weren't up in that time, we'd never see light again.

I don't remember much about what happened after that. I slept and woke every hour to operate the scrubber. I was so tired I couldn't think straight. I couldn't tell what was real and what was a nightmare. Did I wake just now and turn on the scrubber? Was it just a dream?

I fell asleep again. I shut out the bitter cold and the foul air. It would have been easy to switch off the alarm and sleep for ever. But something made me fight. I thought about my wife and family. I thought about all the people who were risking their lives to save us. They hadn't given up on us. I couldn't give up on them.

The radio jolted me awake. A message from Voyager to the other mini-sub. 'Voyager to Pisces 2. You're ten metres down. Everything's okay.'

I could hardly believe my ears. Pisces 2 was on its way down to us! It was now 4.30am on Saturday

1 September. Pisces 2 found us very quickly. Our small world was suddenly flooded with light. We couldn't believe it. It all happened so quickly.

Pisces 2 came to rest a few metres away from us. It waited for the clouds of mud to settle, then fixed a line to us. It made its way back to the surface.

Next the CURV came down. It fixed another line to us. Now there were two very strong lines between us and Voyager. At 11 o'clock on Saturday morning we got the call. 'Voyager to Pisces 3. We start the lift at 11.30.'

I remember thinking, now things are going to get tricky. This is the risky bit. What if we get half-way up and the lines snap? It sounds funny, I know, but all I wanted was to go to sleep. Down there, on the seabed, I could sleep. I could forget about the risks, blot them out.

We turned on the scrubber and let out a blast of oxygen. Our heads were aching and we were numb with cold. But we would soon be on our way at last.

I thought of our ship, Voyager, far above us. Between it and us were two strong lines. It wasn't going to let us sink again.

I looked around at the cramped space that had been our home for three days. 'What a mess,' I thought. Then I laughed. As if it mattered. As if anyone would care.

We looked at each other and smiled. We held hands. The numbers on the depth gauge twitched. We were moving. We were going home!

The lifting lines pulled us free of the mud. We began to swing to and fro. We were thrown about like clothes inside a washing machine. All we could do was hang on – and pray.

9

We were 100 metres from the surface. We'd come to a halt. I panicked. I radioed Voyager. 'Pisces 3 to Voyager. What's happening? Why have we stopped?'

There was a pause. Then the radio crackled into life. 'Voyager to Pisces 3. We have a problem.'

Fear gripped me. Had one of the lines snapped? If both lines broke we'd sink like a stone again. Then I remembered. One of our tanks was full of water. Voyager was having to lift our weight and a tonne of water to the surface.

I spoke to Voyager again. I tried to sound calm. 'Pisces 3 to Voyager. What's the problem? Are we too heavy?'

'No. It's not the weight. The lines are tangled. Hang on. Everything's under control.'

It seemed like an age before the lines were freed. Now we were moving upwards again. We got closer to the surface. Our hearts lifted. We could see daylight. And there, above our heads, were the two lines – our link with Voyager.

We stopped again. What could it be now? What else could go wrong?

Voyager radioed. 'Sorry, Pisces 3. The weather up here is very bad. We're being thrown about like a cork. The wind and waves are too strong to risk a lift.'

I radioed back. 'Pisces 3 to Voyager. What's the plan?'

'We're going to lower you to 30 metres. Then we'll send divers down with a third line.'

'A third line?' I asked.

'Yes, Pisces 3. Divers will bring down a very strong line. Thick enough to lift the Titanic. We're taking no chances. We've got you up so far. We don't want to lose you now.'

Although divers can work safely at 30 metres, it was still a risky job. The sea was very rough. The lifting rope was heavy. The divers struggled to fix it to our sub. It was a long time before the lift could go ahead.

Slowly we rose through the sea once more. Daylight flooded through the water and changed it from black to pale green. At just after 1 o'clock, Pisces 3 broke the surface. I looked at the gauge on the oxygen bottle. We had only 20 minutes left! We'd escaped just in time.

I heard the hatch clang. A rush of fresh air came into the sub. Three pairs of arms reached in and pulled Roger out.

I crawled out after him. We'd survived. We'd made it. Against all the odds, we were alive.

***

Over 250 people took part in the rescue of Pisces 3. It is the longest and deepest rescue of its kind to date. Nobody has ever been rescued from that depth before or since.

Roger Chapman and Roger Mallinson don't think of themselves as 'brave'. They'd survived because they cared for one another. The skill and bravery of the rescue team kept them going. And the thoughts of families and friends who'd spent sleepless nights willing them to come home.

The author interviewed Roger Mallinson for this book.